ENGLAND

WORLD ADVENTURES

BY STEFFI CAVELL-CLARKE

KidHaven
PUBLISHING

Published in 2019 by
KidHaven Publishing, an Imprint of Greenhaven Publishing, LLC
353 3rd Avenue, Suite 255, New York, NY 10010

© 2019 Booklife Publishing

This edition is published by arrangement with Booklife Publishing.

Designer: Matt Rumbelow
Editor: Charlie Ogden
Writer: Steffi Cavell-Clarke

Cataloging-in-Publication Data

Names: Cavell-Clarke, Steffi.
Title: England / Steffi Cavell-Clarke.
Description: New York : KidHaven Publishing, 2019. | Series: World adventures | Includes index.
Identifiers: ISBN 9781534526129 (pbk.) | 9781534526112 (library bound) | ISBN 9781534526136 (6 pack) | ISBN 9781534526143 (ebook)
Subjects: LCSH: England–Juvenile literature. | Great Britain–Juvenile literature.
Classification: LCC DA27.5 C38 2019 | DDC 942–dc23

Printed in the United States of America

CPSIA compliance information: Batch # BS18KL: For further information contact Greenhaven Publishing LLC, New York, New York at 1-844-317-7404.

CONTENTS

Words in **red** can be found in the glossary on page 24.

WHERE IS ENGLAND?

England is a country that is part of the United Kingdom. The United Kingdom includes three other countries called Scotland, Wales, and Northern Ireland.

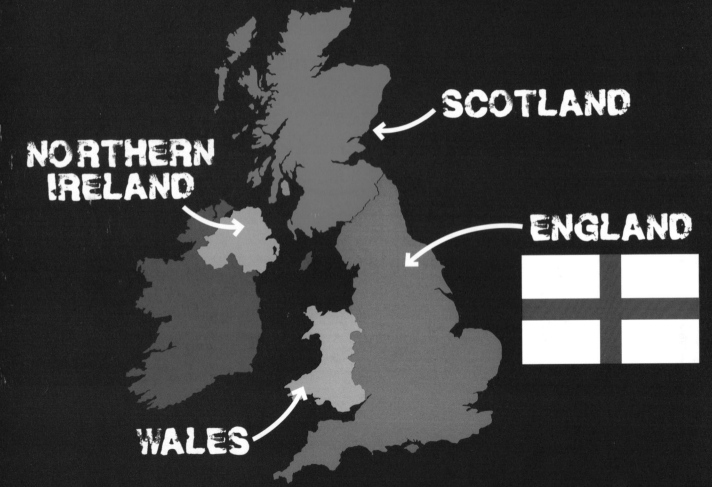

SCOTLAND

NORTHERN IRELAND

ENGLAND

WALES

The **population** of England is over 53 million people. Most of the people living in England speak the English language.

The capital city of England is London.

WEATHER AND LANDSCAPE

The weather in England changes with the seasons. It often gets hotter in the summer and colder in the winter.

SUMMER

WINTER

There are many different types of landscapes across England. There are **coastlines**, forests, rivers, and lakes.

The largest lake in England is Lake Windermere.

LAKE WINDERMERE, ENGLAND

CLOTHING

English people usually wear **modern** clothing, such as jeans and T-shirts.

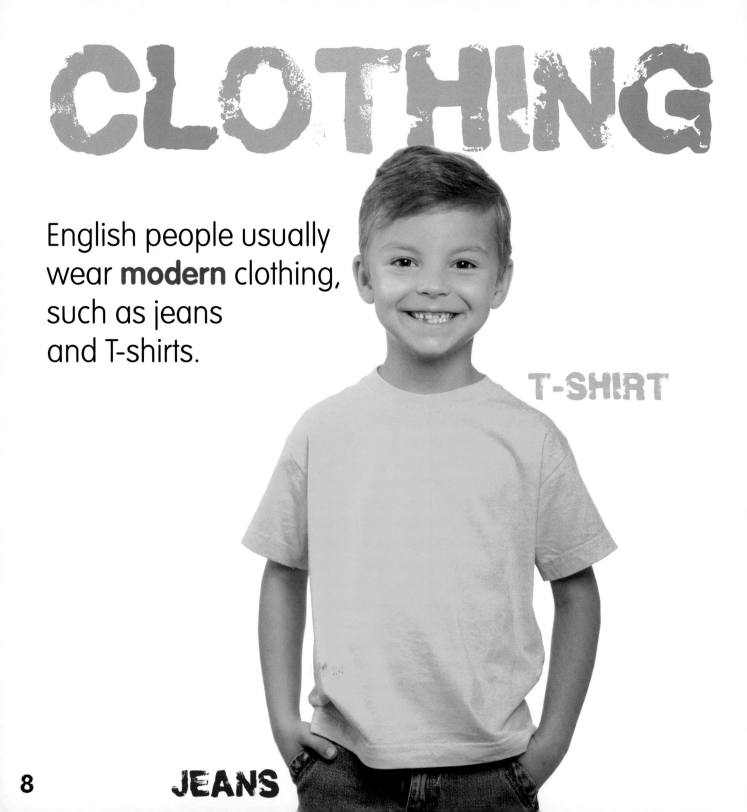

T-SHIRT

JEANS

In England, it is **traditional** for a bride to wear a white dress when she gets married. The men usually wear suits and their guests wear fancy clothing, too.

A bride wearing a wedding dress.

SUIT

RELIGION

The **religion** with the most followers in England is Christianity. A Christian place of **worship** is called a church.

There are over 50,000 churches in England.

There are many people in England that follow other religions, such as Islam and Hinduism. There are also people who do not follow any religion.

FOOD

Fish and chips (french fries) is a popular meal in England. The fish is covered in batter and is often served with mushy peas.

FRIED FISH

The Victoria sponge cake is a traditional cake in England. The filling is made from jam and cream.

AT SCHOOL

Children in England start going to school when they are four years old. They usually leave school when they are 18 years old.

At school, children learn math, science, geography, and English. Many children also go to after-school clubs and play sports, such as soccer.

AT HOME

Many people in England live in large cities. Most cities have tall buildings with apartments for people to live in.

In towns and villages, most people live in houses. Many houses have gardens with trees and flowers.

FAMILIES

Many children in England live with their parents and **siblings**. Lots of families live close to other family members, such as grandparents.

Many English families like to get together to celebrate special occasions, such as weddings and birthdays.

SPORTS

One of the most popular sports in England is soccer. Soccer is played by two teams who try to kick a ball into each other's net.

London has held the Olympic Games three times, and the last time was in 2012. Many of the best **athletes** from around the world went to London to take part in the games.

FUN FACTS

The average person from England drinks over 800 cups of tea each year!

How to make a cup of tea:

1. Boil water in a kettle
2. Put a tea bag in a mug
3. Pour the hot water into the mug
4. Add some milk
5. To make it sweeter, you can add some sugar

Ask an adult to help you!

The British Royal Family live in Buckingham Palace in London, England. At Christmastime, they usually visit their other home in Sandringham, Norfolk.

BUCKINGHAM PALACE

SANDRINGHAM

GLOSSARY

athletes	people who are very good at sport
coastlines	areas of land that meet the sea
modern	something from recent or present times
population	number of people living in a place
religion	the belief in and worship of a god or gods
siblings	brothers and sisters
traditional	something that has been happening for a long time
worship	a religious act, such as praying

INDEX

Photocredits: Abbreviations: l-left, r-right, b-bottom, t-top, c-center, m-middle.
Front Cover - Veronica Louro, bg – Remistudio. 1 - Remistudio. 2 – JeniFoto. 3 - Veronica Louro. 5 – S.Borisov. 6 – Rtimages. 7 – crazychris84. 8 - Andrei Shumskiy. 9 - Ollyy. 10 - Martin Fowler. 11 t - Saida Shigapova, b - Dipak Shelare. 12 - neil langan. 13 - neil langan. 14 - michaeljung. 15 – holbox. 16 - Sean Pavone. 17 - Paolo Gianti. 18 - India Picture. 19 - Oksana Kuzmina. 20 t – Brocreative, b – wavebreakmedia. 21 - MrPics. 22 – antoniodiaz. 23 t - Bucchi Francesco, b - Capture Light. Images are courtesy of Shutterstock.com, unless stated otherwise. With thanks to Getty Images, Thinkstock Photo and iStockphoto.